EMMANUEL JOSEPH

The Universal Melody, How Music Bridges Neuroscience and Cultural Identity

Copyright © 2025 by Emmanuel Joseph

All rights reserved. No part of this publication may be reproduced, stored or transmitted in any form or by any means, electronic, mechanical, photocopying, recording, scanning, or otherwise without written permission from the publisher. It is illegal to copy this book, post it to a website, or distribute it by any other means without permission.

First edition

This book was professionally typeset on Reedsy.
Find out more at reedsy.com

Contents

1	Chapter 1: The Beginnings of Sound	1
2	Chapter 2: The Neuroscience of Music	3
3	Chapter 3: Cultural Identity and Music	5
4	Chapter 4: Music as a Social Connector	7
5	Chapter 5: The Healing Power of Music	9
6	Chapter 6: Music and Memory	11
7	Chapter 7: Emotional Resonance of Music	13
8	Chapter 8: Cognitive Development and Music	15
9	Chapter 9: Music in Multicultural Societies	17
10	Chapter 10: Music and Identity Formation	19
11	Chapter 11: Music and Mental Health	21
12	Chapter 12: The Universal Melody	23
13	Chapter 13: Music and Spirituality	24
14	Chapter 14: Music and Creativity	26
15	Chapter 15: The Future of Music	28

1

Chapter 1: The Beginnings of Sound

From the earliest human civilizations, music has always been a profound thread woven into the fabric of existence. Ancient tribes hummed, drummed, and chanted in rituals, using sound to communicate and celebrate. It became a powerful form of expression, transcending the limitations of spoken language. The babbling brooks, rustling leaves, and the rhythmic cadence of footsteps—all were early forms of music, echoing through the aeons, nurturing a primal connection with the world around us.

Over time, music evolved alongside humanity, branching out into diverse cultures and taking myriad forms. The simple beating of a drum transformed into the sophisticated compositions of classical symphonies and the vibrant beats of modern pop. Every culture, from the indigenous tribes of Africa to the ancient Greeks, developed unique musical styles that reflected their beliefs, histories, and identities. This chapter explores the origins of music, tracing its journey from primitive sounds to the complex, emotive art form we cherish today.

In parallel, the study of music within the framework of neuroscience began to unveil how deeply embedded music is within the human brain. Early neuroscientists discovered that the brain's response to music could be mapped, revealing how melodies and rhythms light up neural pathways, much like how a painter fills a canvas with vibrant colors. The connections forged by these studies opened new vistas in understanding how music shapes our minds and emotions.

By understanding the origins and evolution of music, we can begin to comprehend the profound impact it has on our brains and cultures. The deep-seated connection between music and the human experience underscores its importance in shaping our identities and communities. As we delve deeper into this book, we will explore the fascinating intersections of music, neuroscience, and cultural identity, unraveling the universal melody that unites us all.

2

Chapter 2: The Neuroscience of Music

Music is often described as a universal language, and neuroscientists have been captivated by its power to evoke emotions and memories. The brain's auditory cortex plays a pivotal role in processing musical sounds, breaking them down into components like pitch, rhythm, and timbre. This sophisticated analysis allows us to experience music not just as a sequence of notes, but as a rich tapestry of emotion and meaning.

When we listen to music, various brain regions work in harmony, akin to an orchestra performing a symphony. The hippocampus, responsible for memory formation, links melodies to personal experiences, while the amygdala, the brain's emotional center, processes the emotional impact of the music. Additionally, the motor cortex is activated, even when we're simply listening to a rhythm, which explains why we often find ourselves tapping our feet or swaying to the beat.

Neuroscientific research has also revealed that music has therapeutic potential. For example, patients with neurological disorders like Parkinson's disease have shown improvement in motor functions through rhythmic auditory stimulation. Similarly, music therapy has been used to aid in the rehabilitation of stroke patients and those suffering from mental health conditions, demonstrating its profound healing capabilities.

Through understanding the neuroscience of music, we gain insight into

THE UNIVERSAL MELODY, HOW MUSIC BRIDGES NEUROSCIENCE AND CULTURAL IDENTITY

why it resonates so deeply with us. The intricate dance between brain regions as they process and respond to music highlights the extraordinary capacity of our minds to find meaning and connection in sound. As we continue our exploration, we will see how these neuroscientific insights dovetail with the cultural aspects of music, revealing the intricate ways in which it shapes our identities.

3

Chapter 3: Cultural Identity and Music

Music is a potent symbol of cultural identity, reflecting the values, traditions, and histories of communities. It acts as a repository of cultural memory, preserving stories and customs that define a people. The lullabies sung by mothers to their children, the chants of warriors before battle, and the songs of celebration and mourning all contribute to a culture's sonic landscape, creating a shared sense of belonging and continuity.

Different cultures have developed unique musical styles and instruments, often influenced by their geography, history, and social structures. For instance, the pentatonic scales of East Asian music reflect the philosophical and aesthetic principles of the region, while the complex rhythms of African drumming embody communal participation and storytelling. These musical traditions not only entertain but also educate, transmitting cultural knowledge and values across generations.

In multicultural societies, music serves as a bridge between diverse groups, fostering understanding and unity. It has the power to transcend linguistic and cultural barriers, enabling people to connect on an emotional level. Festivals, concerts, and other musical events often become spaces where cultural exchange and dialogue occur, promoting mutual respect and appreciation.

Examining the role of music in cultural identity helps us appreciate the rich tapestry of human diversity. It reveals how music can both reflect and shape the values and aspirations of communities. By understanding these connections, we can better appreciate the role of music in fostering a sense of belonging and unity, both within and across cultures. As we delve further, we'll explore how music's cultural dimensions intersect with its neuroscientific foundations.

4

Chapter 4: Music as a Social Connector

Throughout history, music has played a crucial role in bringing people together. From communal gatherings around a campfire to massive music festivals, shared musical experiences create bonds and foster a sense of community. The act of making music together, whether in a choir, band, or drum circle, requires cooperation and collaboration, strengthening social ties and fostering mutual respect.

Music's ability to evoke emotions and memories makes it a powerful tool for social cohesion. Songs and anthems often become symbols of collective identity, rallying people around a common cause or shared experience. For example, protest songs have galvanized social movements, providing a soundtrack to calls for justice and change. Similarly, national anthems and folk songs evoke feelings of patriotism and cultural pride, reinforcing a sense of belonging.

In modern times, the advent of digital technology and social media has expanded the reach of music, allowing it to connect people across the globe. Online platforms enable musicians to share their work with a global audience, fostering cross-cultural exchanges and collaborations. Virtual concerts and livestreamed performances have created new opportunities for communal musical experiences, even in the face of physical distance.

By examining music's role as a social connector, we can better understand its potential to bridge divides and foster unity. It highlights the importance of creating spaces where people can come together through music, celebrating both their unique cultural identities and their shared humanity. As we continue our exploration, we'll delve into the therapeutic aspects of music and its impact on individual well-being.

5

Chapter 5: The Healing Power of Music

Music has long been recognized for its therapeutic properties, offering solace and healing in times of distress. Ancient cultures used music in healing rituals and ceremonies, believing in its power to restore balance and harmony. Today, music therapy is a well-established field, with practitioners using music to address a wide range of physical, emotional, and cognitive issues.

The neurological basis of music's therapeutic effects lies in its ability to engage multiple brain regions simultaneously. This holistic engagement can help alleviate symptoms of various conditions, from depression and anxiety to chronic pain and neurological disorders. For instance, music therapy has been shown to improve motor function in patients with Parkinson's disease and to reduce anxiety and stress in cancer patients undergoing treatment.

In addition to its direct therapeutic benefits, music also promotes overall well-being by enhancing mood, reducing stress, and fostering a sense of connection. Listening to or creating music can provide an emotional outlet, allowing individuals to process and express their feelings. Group music-making activities, such as choir singing or drumming circles, create opportunities for social interaction and support, further enhancing the therapeutic experience.

The healing power of music underscores its profound impact on our lives. By understanding the mechanisms behind its therapeutic effects, we can harness music's potential to improve individual and collective well-being. As we delve deeper into the connections between music, neuroscience, and cultural identity, we will continue to uncover the ways in which music enriches our lives and unites us as a global community.

6

Chapter 6: Music and Memory

Music has a unique ability to evoke memories, transporting us back to specific moments in time. This phenomenon is rooted in the brain's intricate network of connections between the auditory cortex, hippocampus, and other regions involved in memory processing. When we hear a familiar song, it can trigger vivid recollections and emotions, often more powerfully than other sensory cues.

Research has shown that music can be a valuable tool in memory rehabilitation, particularly for individuals with Alzheimer's disease and other forms of dementia. Patients who struggle to recall recent events or recognize loved ones can often remember and sing along to songs from their past. This remarkable ability highlights the resilience of musical memory and its potential to improve quality of life for those with cognitive impairments.

In addition to its therapeutic applications, music also plays a role in preserving cultural memory. Traditional songs, lullabies, and folk tunes carry the stories and histories of communities, passing down knowledge and values through generations. These musical memories contribute to a shared sense of identity and continuity, reinforcing the bonds between individuals and their cultural heritage.

By exploring the connections between music and memory, we gain insight into the powerful ways in which music shapes our experiences and identities. It reveals the deep-seated connections between our past, present, and future, highlighting the enduring impact of music on our lives. As we continue our journey, we will delve into the ways in which music influences emotional and cognitive development across the lifespan.

7

Chapter 7: Emotional Resonance of Music

Music has an unparalleled ability to evoke and modulate emotions, making it a powerful tool for emotional expression and regulation. The brain's response to music involves a complex interplay of neural circuits, including those involved in emotion, reward, and arousal. This intricate network allows music to tap into our deepest feelings, from joy and excitement to sadness and nostalgia.

Different musical elements, such as melody, harmony, and rhythm, can evoke distinct emotional responses. For example, a major key and an upbeat tempo are often associated with feelings of happiness and excitement, while a minor key and a slower tempo can evoke sadness or melancholy. The brain's reward system, which includes the release of dopamine, plays a crucial role in the pleasure we derive from music, reinforcing our emotional connections to it.

The ability of music to convey and evoke emotions is not limited to personal experiences; it also reflects the collective emotional landscape of cultures and societies. Cultural norms and traditions shape the ways in which music is created and interpreted, influencing the emotional messages conveyed through melodies and lyrics. For instance, the joyful rhythms of a samba or the mournful strains of a lament can communicate powerful cultural emotions, resonating deeply with those who share that cultural heritage.

Understanding the emotional resonance of music provides valuable insights into its role in our lives. It highlights the ways in which music can both reflect and shape our emotions, offering a means of expression and connection that transcends words. As we continue our exploration, we will delve into the cognitive development influenced by music and its role in enhancing learning and creativity.

8

Chapter 8: Cognitive Development and Music

Music plays a significant role in cognitive development, particularly during childhood. Engaging with music from a young age can enhance various cognitive skills, including language development, mathematical abilities, and spatial reasoning. Research has shown that children who receive musical training often perform better in academic subjects, demonstrating the far-reaching benefits of musical education.

The link between music and language development is particularly strong. Both music and language rely on auditory processing, rhythm, and pattern recognition. Exposure to music can improve phonological awareness, which is essential for reading and language comprehension. Singing and playing instruments also promote fine motor skills and coordination, further supporting cognitive development.

Music's impact on cognitive development extends beyond childhood. Lifelong engagement with music can contribute to cognitive resilience and delay age-related cognitive decline. Activities such as playing an instrument, singing in a choir, or even actively listening to music can stimulate the brain, keeping neural pathways active and promoting mental agility.

Exploring the connections between music and cognitive development underscores the importance of incorporating music into educational and daily life. It reveals how music can enhance learning and creativity, providing a valuable tool for cognitive growth across the lifespan. As we continue our journey, we will delve into the ways in which music influences social interactions and fosters a sense of community.

9

Chapter 9: Music in Multicultural Societies

In multicultural societies, music serves as a bridge between diverse cultural groups, fostering mutual understanding and appreciation. The exchange of musical traditions can lead to the creation of new, hybrid genres that reflect the rich tapestry of cultural influences. This blending of musical styles not only enriches the cultural landscape but also promotes dialogue and collaboration between different communities.

One notable example of musical fusion is jazz, which emerged in the early 20th century in the United States. Jazz drew on African rhythms, European harmonic structures, and various other influences, creating a genre that resonated with a wide audience and became a symbol of cultural integration. Similarly, genres like reggae, hip-hop, and electronic music have evolved through the blending of different cultural elements, reflecting the dynamic nature of multicultural societies.

Music festivals and events in multicultural societies often showcase a diverse array of musical traditions, providing opportunities for cross-cultural exchange and celebration. These gatherings create spaces where people can come together to share their heritage and learn from one another, fostering a sense of unity and belonging.

By examining the role of music in multicultural societies, we gain insight into its potential to bridge divides and foster a sense of global community. It highlights the importance of preserving and celebrating cultural diversity while promoting understanding and collaboration. As we continue our exploration, we will delve into the ways in which music shapes individual and collective identities.

10

Chapter 10: Music and Identity Formation

Music plays a crucial role in the formation of individual and collective identities. The genres, artists, and songs that we connect with often reflect our personal values, experiences, and aspirations. Our musical preferences can serve as a form of self-expression, communicating aspects of our identity to others and helping us navigate the complexities of social interactions.

For many people, music is closely tied to significant life events and personal milestones. The songs that accompany our happiest moments, our struggles, and our triumphs become part of our personal narrative, shaping our sense of self. Similarly, the music we listen to during different stages of our lives can reflect and influence our emotional and psychological development.

Collective identity is also shaped by music, as communities and cultures use music to express shared values and experiences. National anthems, folk songs, and cultural festivals all contribute to a sense of belonging and continuity, reinforcing the bonds between individuals and their cultural heritage. Music can also serve as a tool for social and political movements, galvanizing collective action and inspiring change.

By exploring the connections between music and identity formation, we gain a deeper understanding of the ways in which music influences our lives. It reveals how music can both reflect and shape our individual and collective identities, providing a powerful means of expression and connection. As we continue our journey, we will delve into the ways in which music influences emotional regulation and mental health.

11

Chapter 11: Music and Mental Health

Music has a profound impact on mental health, offering a means of emotional expression, regulation, and healing. Listening to or creating music can provide an emotional outlet, allowing individuals to process and express their feelings in a safe and supportive environment. Music can also serve as a form of self-care, helping to reduce stress, anxiety, and depression.

The therapeutic effects of music are supported by research in the field of music therapy. Music therapists use music to address a wide range of mental health issues, from mood disorders to trauma and grief. Techniques such as songwriting, improvisation, and guided imagery can help individuals explore and process their emotions, build coping skills, and improve overall well-being.

In addition to its direct therapeutic benefits, music also promotes social connection and support, which are essential for mental health. Group music-making activities, such as choir singing or drum circles, create opportunities for social interaction and a sense of belonging. These communal experiences can help reduce feelings of isolation and foster a supportive community.

By examining the connections between music and mental health, we gain insight into the powerful ways in which music can enhance emotional well-being. It highlights the importance of incorporating music into mental health care and self-care practices. As we conclude our exploration, we will reflect on the universal melody that unites us all and the enduring impact of music on our lives.

12

Chapter 12: The Universal Melody

Throughout this book, we have explored the profound connections between music, neuroscience, and cultural identity. From the earliest sounds of human civilization to the therapeutic applications of music in modern times, we have seen how music transcends boundaries and unites us in a shared human experience.

The universal melody of music resonates deeply within our brains, lighting up neural pathways and evoking emotions, memories, and connections. It serves as a bridge between diverse cultures, fostering understanding and unity. Music's role in cognitive development, emotional regulation, and mental health underscores its importance in shaping our lives and well-being.

As we reflect on the universal melody that weaves through our existence, we are reminded of the power of music to connect us to ourselves, to each other, and to the world around us. It is a testament to the beauty and resilience of the human spirit, a source of joy, healing, and inspiration.

May we continue to cherish and celebrate the universal melody of music, recognizing its profound impact on our lives and its potential to bring us closer together. Let the music play on, guiding us in our journey of discovery, connection, and growth.

13

Chapter 13: Music and Spirituality

Throughout history, music has played a significant role in spiritual and religious practices. From the chanting of mantras in Hinduism to the hymns sung in Christian churches, music has been used to connect with the divine, elevate the soul, and create a sense of transcendence. The rhythmic patterns and melodies in sacred music are believed to have the power to induce meditative states, deepen spiritual experiences, and foster a sense of communion with a higher power.

Different cultures and religions have developed unique musical traditions that reflect their spiritual beliefs and practices. For instance, the intricate patterns of Gregorian chants in Christianity create a serene and contemplative atmosphere, while the drumming and singing in African spiritual rituals invoke ancestral spirits and facilitate communication with the divine. These musical expressions serve as a conduit for spiritual experiences, bridging the gap between the physical and the metaphysical.

The neuroscientific study of music and spirituality reveals how deeply intertwined these experiences are with our brain's functioning. Listening to or participating in sacred music can activate brain regions associated with reward, emotion, and introspection, creating a sense of spiritual fulfillment and connectedness. The shared experience of communal worship through music also fosters a sense of unity and belonging, reinforcing the bonds within religious communities.

CHAPTER 13: MUSIC AND SPIRITUALITY

By exploring the connections between music and spirituality, we gain insight into the profound ways in which music shapes our spiritual lives. It highlights the power of music to elevate the human spirit, providing a source of solace, inspiration, and transcendence. As we continue our journey, we will delve into the ways in which music influences creativity and innovation.

14

Chapter 14: Music and Creativity

Music has long been associated with creativity and innovation, both in the arts and beyond. Engaging with music, whether through listening, composing, or performing, can stimulate the brain's creative processes, fostering new ideas and perspectives. The improvisational nature of jazz, the experimental sounds of electronic music, and the poetic lyrics of songwriting all exemplify the creative potential of music.

The neuroscience of creativity reveals that music engages multiple brain regions involved in divergent thinking, problem-solving, and emotional expression. Musical improvisation, for instance, activates the prefrontal cortex, which is responsible for decision-making and self-expression. This engagement of the brain's creative centers allows musicians to explore new musical ideas and push the boundaries of their art.

Music's influence on creativity extends beyond the realm of music itself. Studies have shown that listening to music can enhance cognitive flexibility, improving the ability to think outside the box and generate innovative solutions. This creative boost is not limited to the arts; it can also benefit fields such as science, technology, and business, where innovative thinking is essential.

By examining the connections between music and creativity, we gain a deeper understanding of the ways in which music can inspire and nurture innovation. It highlights the importance of incorporating music into our lives and work, providing a valuable tool for creative expression and problem-solving. As we conclude our exploration, we will reflect on the future of music and its enduring impact on humanity.

15

Chapter 15: The Future of Music

As we look to the future, the role of music in our lives is likely to continue evolving, shaped by technological advancements and cultural shifts. Digital technology has already transformed the way we create, share, and experience music, making it more accessible and diverse than ever before. Virtual reality, artificial intelligence, and other emerging technologies hold the potential to further revolutionize the musical landscape.

The rise of virtual reality (VR) offers new possibilities for immersive musical experiences, allowing listeners to step inside a virtual concert hall or create music in a three-dimensional space. AI-powered tools can assist musicians in composing, arranging, and producing music, opening up new avenues for creativity and collaboration. These technologies can also personalize music recommendations, creating tailored listening experiences that resonate with individual preferences and moods.

In addition to technological advancements, the future of music will be shaped by ongoing cultural and social changes. As our world becomes increasingly interconnected, the blending of musical traditions from different cultures will continue to inspire new genres and styles. This cross-cultural exchange will enrich the global musical landscape, fostering understanding and unity among diverse communities.

As we reflect on the future of music, we are reminded of its enduring impact on humanity. Music will continue to be a source of joy, healing, and inspiration, connecting us to ourselves and to one another. It is a testament to the resilience and creativity of the human spirit, a universal melody that transcends time and space.

The Universal Melody: How Music Bridges Neuroscience and Cultural Identity

Dive into the harmonious interplay between the brain and music, and uncover the rich tapestry of cultural identity. "The Universal Melody" takes readers on a captivating journey through the origins of sound, the profound impact of music on our neural circuits, and the powerful role it plays in shaping cultural identities.

This book delves into the roots of music, tracing its evolution from the rhythmic beating of ancient drums to the complex compositions of modern symphonies. Discover how music activates diverse regions of the brain, evoking emotions, memories, and healing. Explore the therapeutic potential of music, its significance in cognitive development, and its ability to foster social cohesion and understanding.

From traditional folk songs to contemporary fusion genres, "The Universal Melody" celebrates the diverse musical traditions that enrich our global community. Through the lens of neuroscience and cultural studies, this book illuminates the universal language of music that connects us all, transcending boundaries and uniting us in a shared human experience.

Whether you're a music enthusiast, a curious mind, or a seeker of cultural understanding, this book offers valuable insights into the profound ways music shapes our lives and identities. Join us in exploring the universal melody that resonates deeply within our souls and across the world.

www.ingramcontent.com/pod-product-compliance
Lightning Source LLC
LaVergne TN
LVHW020741090526
838202LV00057BA/6162